TILLS™

TEST OF INTEGRATED LANGUAGE & LITERACY SKILLS™

Student Response Form

Student name: ______________________________ Test date: ______________

I0737603

DO NOT BREAK.

These forms are not sold individually. They are available only as a set. Resellers should not open shrink-wrapped sets.

ISBN-13: 978-1-59857-910-9
ISBN-10: 1-59857-910-X

90000>

9 781598 579109

Manufactured in the U.S.A.

SUBTEST 5: Nonword Spelling (NWSpell)

Practice Items

____

____

Test Items

1. ______________________________
2. ______________________________
3. ______________________________
4. ______________________________
5. ______________________________
6. ______________________________
7. ______________________________
8. ______________________________
9. ______________________________
10. ______________________________
11. ______________________________
12. ______________________________
13. ______________________________
14. ______________________________
15. ______________________________
16. ______________________________
17. ______________________________
18. ______________________________
19. ______________________________
20. ______________________________
21. ______________________________
22. ______________________________
23. ______________________________
24. ______________________________

1.	**"What I Did on My Summer Vacation" is the topic the teacher makes her class write about the first day of school every year. When school started a month ago, the teacher gave her usual first writing assignment.**			
a.	Was "The Middle East" the first writing assignment?	Yes	No	Maybe
b.	Did all of the students take a trip on their summer vacation?	Yes	No	Maybe
c.	Did the teacher ask her class to write about their summer vacations?	Yes	No	Maybe

2.	**Last summer, Renaldo and Jake had fun in summer school learning new things. Photography was Renaldo's favorite class; in fact, the picture that Renaldo took of his friend Jake won the summer school prize.**			
a.	Did Jake win the summer school prize?	Yes	No	Maybe
b.	Did Jake take a picture?	Yes	No	Maybe
c.	Did both boys have a good time in summer school?	Yes	No	Maybe

3.	**Anna was excited when she thought about playing with her new hamster every day. However, she was surprised when she discovered that her hamster sleeps all day and runs on his wheel all night.**			
a.	Does Anna's hamster sleep all night?	Yes	No	Maybe
b.	Did Anna expect her hamster to sleep all day before she brought him home?	Yes	No	Maybe
c.	Does Anna's hamster keep her awake all night?	Yes	No	Maybe

4.	**All his friends thought that Carlos looked better before he had his hair cut by Juan.**			
a.	Is Juan a barber?	Yes	No	Maybe
b.	Did Carlos's friends think Juan's haircut improved Carlos's looks?	Yes	No	Maybe
c.	Did Carlos like his new haircut?	Yes	No	Maybe

5.	**One morning Susan got up too late to catch the school bus. She thought that she would be late for school, but her mother got her there on time.**			
a.	Did Susan miss the bus?	Yes	No	Maybe
b.	Was it raining that morning?	Yes	No	Maybe
c.	Did Susan expect to miss the start of the school day?	Yes	No	Maybe

6.	**The sport Eddie likes to play best is soccer. He can kick a soccer ball the second farthest in his class and run faster than anybody in his class.**			
a.	Can Eddie kick a soccer ball farther than anyone else in his class?	Yes	No	Maybe
b.	Does Eddie like to play baseball?	Yes	No	Maybe
c.	Does Eddie run the fastest in his class?	Yes	No	Maybe

7.	**The scientists observed the insects closely over a 24-hour period, hoping to study their swarming behavior. At that point, the scientists concluded that the insects had been prevented from swarming because of the unusual atmospheric conditions.**			
a.	Did the insects swarm during the observation period?	Yes	No	Maybe
b.	Can atmospheric conditions influence the swarming of insects?	Yes	No	Maybe
c.	Did the scientists draw a conclusion even though the study did not go exactly as planned?	Yes	No	Maybe

SUBTEST 8: **Following Directions (FD)**

Practice Items

1. 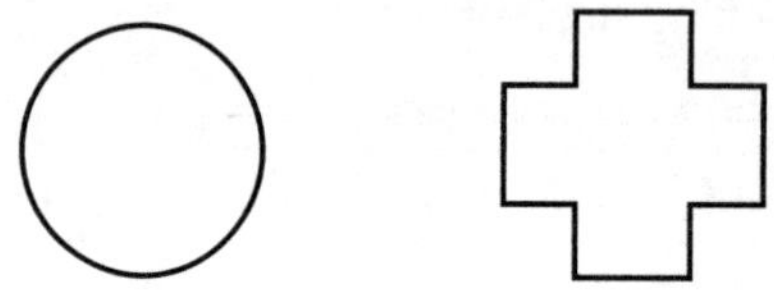

2. 

Test Items

1. 

2. 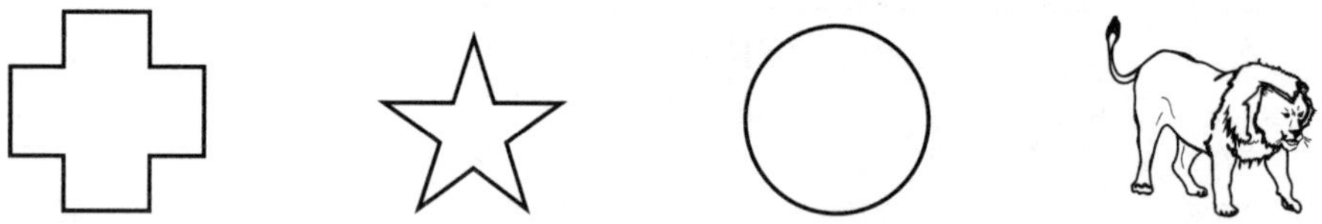

3. 

4. 

5. 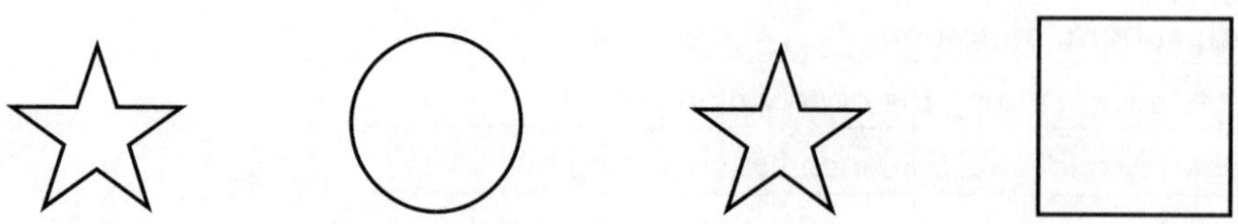

6. 

7. 

8. 

9. 3 X W 7 B

10. 

11. 

12. 

13. 

14. 

15. 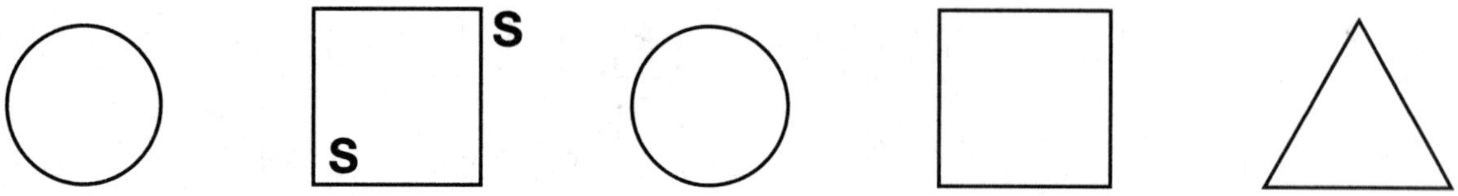

16. 

17. 

18. 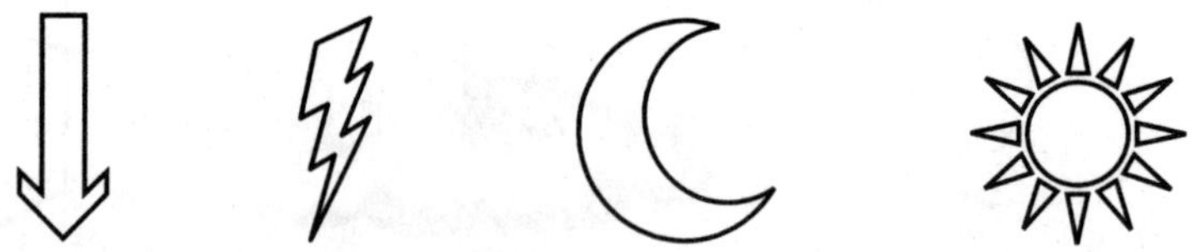

19. E 88 e 20 S 16

20. 2 f a C F

Sample Rewritten Story

A little brown-and-white dog almost
got hit by a car in front of our school.
He was scared, but he was okay.

Turn the page to begin writing.

SUBTEST 12: **Written Expression (WE)**

Student's Written Story